What I Wish I Knew When I Was in ... College

77 Secrets **EVERY** Student Needs to Know about Succeeding in School, Leadership, Life, and a Career

By Jerry Franklin Poe

Published by Poetential Unlimited LLC

Printed in the United States of America

ISBN: 978-1-939321-01-5

Warning — Disclaimer

The purpose of this book is to educate and entertain. The author or publisher does not guarantee that anyone following the techniques, suggestions, tips, ideas, or strategies will become successful. The author and publisher shall have neither liability nor responsibility to anyone with respect to any loss or damage caused, or alleged to be caused, directly or indirectly by the information contained in this book.

www.JerryPoe.com

About Jerry Franklin Poe

Jerry Franklin Poe is the founder of Poetential Unlimited LLC, a company designed to train and equip the mind, activate the vision, cultivate the passion, and hone the skills necessary to live life on your terms.

Jerry turned his passion for personal growth and development into a life mission of showing individuals and organizations how to achieve their purpose and goals in life.

As a well known speaker, Jerry has delivered over 2,900 empowering presentations to schools, colleges, and organizations across North America. Jerry has spent the last 14 years working in higher education, leadership consulting, and motivational speaking. Jerry uses real-life experiences, stories, and analogies to educate, equip, inspire, and entertain his audience.

Jerry has authored two books and is a certified life and business coach.

www.JerryPoe.com

Schedule Jerry Franklin Poe to Speak at Your Event
(484) 301-0763
www.JerryPoe.com

Your Ideal Speaker for:
- Conference Keynotes
- Conference Workshops
- Black History Month
- Greek/Panhellenic Events
- Leadership Retreats
- Orientations
- Student Government Programs
- Summer Programs

Top 3 Most Requested Topics:

1. ***What I Wish I Knew About Being a Great Student Leader***
   - How to become a better leader and difference maker on your campus
2. ***What I Wish I Knew About Excelling in School***
   - Ideas that will put you ahead of your class from day one
3. ***What I Wish I Knew About Building a Profitable Career***
   - How to become the employee companies love to hire

Special Bonus
Schedule Jerry and receive 100 FREE BOOKS

Empower and Equip Others!
Share this Book

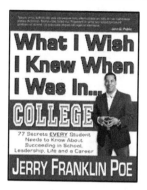

What I Wish I Knew When I Was in ... College

77 Secrets EVERY Student Needs to Know about Succeeding in School, Leadership, Life, and a Career

How great would it be if you were given a manual to guide you through every aspect of your life that lay ahead of you? Give yourself the winning edge. Crack the code to success in school, leadership, life, and a career by reading the tips shared throughout this book. These quick tips are easy to read, understand, and more importantly apply immediately. Go ahead and get started!

Special Quantity Discounts

2 – 20 Books	**$15.00**
21 – 99 Books	**$14.00**
100 – 499 Books	**$13.00**
500 – 999 Books	**$12.00**
1000+ Books	**$11.00**

To Place an Order
Call (484) 301-0763

www.JerryPoe.com

Why I Wrote the Book

"I wish I knew" is a phrase we hear all the time. I know I have said it countless times over the years. I bet you have said it as well. If we had a time machine, we could travel back and enlighten our younger selves. The reality is no one can go back in time. However, I decided to do the next best thing ... share the wisdom of my life experience with the next generation.

My objective is to assist as many young people as possible and help them become well rounded, productive citizens. If I had understood these life lessons, strategies, and suggestions in my youth, I could have saved myself a lot of heartaches and headaches.

I hope you appreciate the information shared throughout this book and apply it to your life.

-JFP

"**Faith is the key to unlock the results you desire.**"

- Jerry Franklin Poe

Secret #1

Pick a Major Based on What Interests You instead of the Amount of Money You Want to Make

One of the biggest mistakes a person can make—if not the biggest mistake a person can make—is picking a major based on the job market and salary you want when you are not passionate about the subject matter. It is very difficult to push yourself to study and sacrifice for a major in which you have no real interest.

Getting a job and making a certain dollar amount are not motivating enough to overcome all the challenges you face as a student.

It is much easier to succeed when you study something you like. When you major in something that interests you, you will have a natural desire to learn more about the topic. (Ultimately you do want to find a way to monetize what you are learning.)

What are you good at? What are you naturally curious about? What have you always been drawn to? What subjects excite you? What do you have a passion for?

It is okay to major in what interests you. It is okay to major in what you like.

"You never achieve real success unless you like what you are doing."

- Dale Carnegie

Secret #2

Look for Solutions

No matter what's going on in your life, no matter what situations you experience, look for the solution. Don't look at the problem.

"How do I solve this problem?" That's one of the questions you must ask yourself, along with "How do I keep going in the midst of this challenge?" and "What can I do to make it work?"

You must be driven by the consequence or outcome. The problem is not stopping you from getting the end result you want. You may have an issue at this moment in time, but do you still deserve to get the result you desire? What are you going to do to achieve that result and keep things moving forward?

Condition your mind to immediately go into solution mode every time you encounter a problem. Do you deal with problems or puzzles? The words you use to describe the obstacles you encounter in life determine your routine.

How do you feel when you hear the word *problem*? How do you feel when you hear the word *puzzle*? Which word prompts you to look for a solution? With a puzzle you focus on finding the answer or putting the pieces together rather than focusing on how challenging the puzzle is. You were taught strategies to solve puzzles.

When you are faced with a problem, always look for a way to solve it. Do not get stuck and dwell on the problem itself.

> *"What happens is not as important as how you react to what happens."*
>
> *- Thaddeus Golas*

Secret #3

Fear Is Natural

Our Deepest Fear Is that We Are Powerful Beyond Measure

Our deepest fear is not that we are inadequate. Our deepest fear is that we are powerful beyond measure. It is our light, not our darkness, that most frightens us. We ask ourselves, who am I to be brilliant, gorgeous, talented and fabulous? Actually, who are you not to be? You are a child of God. Your playing small doesn't serve the world. We were born to make manifest the glory of God that is within us. It's not just in some of us; it's in everyone. And as we let our own light shine, we unconsciously give other people permission to do the same. As we are liberated from our own fear, our presence automatically liberates others.

Marianne Williamson in Return to Love *(Often mistakenly attributed to Nelson Mandela)*

Why is it that our deepest fear is that we are powerful? If we are powerful beyond measure, then we have a responsibility to ourselves and to the world to manifest that power.

We owe it to the One who gave us the power to utilize it. We have to play full out. We have to grow and develop. We have to expand our comfort zone. It would be a disservice not to. For whom much is given much is required, therefore we should feel obligated to make things happen within our lives. We have to create a world full of possibility and unlimited potential. We should feel it is our duty to unlock the potential and greatness inside us. We should want to "leave it all on the mat" as we say in wrestling. We shouldn't hold anything back.

Instead, though, we would rather convince ourselves we are inadequate. Why, do you ask? For the simple reason that it frees us from doing anything, allowing us to live a quiet existence, with no one even knowing we were ever here. We could play small and not make any waves, flying under the radar ... playing it safe ... being comfortable. In the long run this would benefit no one. We would be buried, lying in the grave with our gifts still inside us. Our potential would be untapped.

Think about the time just after a holiday season, when most of us spend lots of quality time, energy, and resources acquiring gifts and presents for our loved ones. We put much thought and love into these gifts and presents. We visualize our loved ones opening the gifts. We see the joy and happiness it will bring them. We see them using and getting value and enjoyment from the gifts we give them. It fills our hearts with joy knowing we are blessing them. Now, the day comes when you give the gifts to them. You cannot wait to see them open the gifts and experience the benefits that come with them. BUT, your loved ones never unwrap the gifts you gave them. Instead, they go outside, dig a hole, and bury the gifts in the ground for safekeeping. How do you feel?

This is actually what most of us do with our lives ...

When are you going to unwrap the gifts you were given?

"Fear does not disappear ... you must become greater than the fear."
– JFP

Secret #4

You Are More than Your Resume

Who you are as a person can outshine your resume. Your personality can make the difference. The resume highlights the tangibles; however, it is up to you throughout the interview process to highlight your intangibles.

What personality traits separate you from the pack?

Intangible Traits

- Organization
- Attitude
- Likeability
- Creativity
- Flexibility
- Teamwork
- Problem-Solving
- Judgment
- Dependability
- Project Management
- Leadership

It is not the resume. It is you.

Secret #5

Use Office Hours and Get to Know Your Professors

Building a relationship with your professors outside the classroom will definitely give you an advantage. It is not wise to look at office hours as an optional thing. Most people do not understand the opportunity they are giving up when they do that. Taking advantage of your professors' office hours enables you to get individual attention, build a rapport with them, and pick their brains.

What better time is there to get the answers to questions you have that you do not want to ask in front of the class?

What better time is there to get their perspective on how they would excel in their own class?

What better time is there to find out what they are expecting from you as a student?

Office hours are not optional. Get the professor and teaching assistant on your side.

www.JerryPoe.com

Secret #6

The Show Must Go On

Successful leaders make things happen. They do not allow mishaps or setbacks to shut down the operation. They find a way to make it happen regardless.

As long as you stay calm and level headed, everyone else will be oblivious to all the chaos going on.

Understanding that the show must go on enables you to get the outcome you are seeking in the midst of chaos.

As a leader you cannot give up and quit. People are depending on you to find a way to accomplish the task.

Never let them see you sweat.

"Adversity reveals genius, prosperity conceals it."

– Horace

Secret #7

Choose Empowering Beliefs

The process of changing a belief can be as easy or hard as we make it. It is important to know that it will take some amount of time for the new belief to become dominant. How much time? The answer to this question may vary from person to person; however, there are things we can do to speed up the process.

Think of a belief as a table. The strength of a table can be determined by its legs. The stronger the legs, the stronger the table; the more legs a table has, the stronger it will be. The legs support the table. Therefore, to make our beliefs stronger and dominant we must support them. How do we support our beliefs? After we choose a belief, there are a few things we can do to support it.

- Facts
- Reasons
- Actions
- Feelings

Find facts that confirm the belief. **Fact** - a thing that has actually happened or that is really true; a thing that has been or is; the state of things as they are; reality; actuality; truth.

Find reasons to endorse the belief. **Reason** - an explanation or justification of an act, idea, etc.

Take actions to reinforce the belief. **Action** - the doing of something; the state of being in motion or of working.

Experience feelings that encourage the belief. **Feelings** - an awareness; consciousness; sensation.

In other words, ask yourself the question: "If the belief were true, what would I do or feel?"

Next, you have to do something. Take action to support your new belief and experience the feeling that action creates. The more you do this, the quicker new beliefs gets locked in.

Develop beliefs that empower you.

"Your mindset establishes the standard for your life." - JFP

Secret #8

Be a Help, Not a Headache

You do not want to be known for causing other people problems, or for being a complainer or criticizer.

There are people who become headaches to their boss. They become headaches to their clients. They become headaches to their coworkers. They become headaches to their business partners. They become headaches to their colleagues.

People do not want to work with you if you cause other people pain.

Be known as a person that is a help rather than a headache. You do not want to be thought about as the one causing problems. You want people to know that if you are there, everything is going to be done right and in order, that they can rely on you to make things happen.

You do not want people thinking, "What am I going to have to fix because he/she is there?" You want people's minds to be at ease when they think about you, to be relaxed because they know things are taken care of.

> *"It is one of the most beautiful compensations of this life that no man can sincerely try to help another without helping himself."*
>
> *- Ralph Waldo Emerson*

Secret #9

What Worked in High School Does Not Always Work in College

The rules of the game are different in college than high school.

In high school you are looked at as a child or a minor.

In college you are looked at as an adult.

The expectations are much different for a minor than an adult. As an adult, people expect you to take more responsibility for yourself. No one is going to hold your hand. No one is going to baby you. The consequences of your actions are different.

Be conscious of the fact that you may have to make adjustments in how you study, how you pick your friends, how you use your time, etc.

Because it worked in high school does not mean it will work in college.

www.JerryPoe.com

Secret #10

Develop a High Tolerance for Frustration

If you want to be a leader, then you must be prepared to handle anything thrown at you. In some cases, things will not always go your way. There will be many moments of frustration. However, the person who can withstand more frustration than others will always win.

When things do not go your way, as a leader what are you going to do?

When times get tough, as a leader what are you going to do?

Are you going to give in?

Are you going to quit?

Or are you going to push through?

What will assist you when it comes to handling the frustrating moments will be learning how to reframe and control your emotions.

Secret #11

Claim Your Victory

1. Live from Possibility, Not Predictability

Let your imagination guide you into the freedom you wish to experience. The safe route is to stay in the predictable lane. However, safety is like bait in a trap: it looks good from the outside, but when you get it, you discover you are now imprisoned in a mediocre life.

2. Speak the Reality You Desire to Experience

What do you say about your life? Your words have the power to create. Are you using them effectively?

3. Act as if It Is Already DONE (Desired Outcome Now Experienced)

Begin to take action that coincides with what you are speaking into existence. Do it with the confidence of a victorious person.

4. Keep Moving Forward—Reverse Is Not an Option

How hard would you fight for your desired outcome if it were a life-or-death situation? Reality check: it is sink or swim, there is no land in sight. What are you going to do?

5. Surrender to the Process and Enjoy the Journey

There is a process we have to go through in order to experience our desired outcome. Do not resist the transformation. The more you resist, the more your current reality will persist.

6. Live Everyday in the NEW (Naturally Embracing Winning)

Win the race you are in today. Learn from your past experiences and move on. Each morning we are reborn to a fresh new day. Live it to the fullest; do not try to relive yesterday today.

7. Rely on Your Inner Strength, Not the Outer

The spirit and soul will continue a lot longer than the body. When the body wants to quit, go deep inside to pull out the power to drive you forward to victory.

Secret #12

Research Them Because They Will Research You

Learn as much as you can about the organization before the interview.

Visit their website. Look them up with the help of a search engine. Find and read articles on the organization. If possible, talk to other people who work there.

During the interview process ask questions about the organization. Also, you might be asked questions to determine how much you know about the organization. If you do the research ahead of time, you will be prepared.

Finding information about the organization is a sign of interest. It indicates you are serious about the opportunity to be a part of their organization.

Show them you care.

Secret #13

Knowing Who the Decision Makers Are Is Not as Important as Them Knowing You

It is great to know who makes the decisions about housing, financial aid, etc. However, if they do not recognize your name or face, knowing them does not matter.

Develop a relationship with those who directly impact your college experience. Introduce yourself to the President, Director of Student Life, Director of Resident Life, Director of Financial Aid, Director of Public Safety, etc. Make appointments to visit their offices a few times a semester to check in and update them on your progress at the institution.

Ask how you can be of assistance to them. When you approach people with a giving attitude rather than a receiving one, they are more willing to help you long term.

You can be another number or a person.

www.JerryPoe.com

Secret #14

Become Audacious

Be daring! Be bold! Be brave!

Set the bar higher because it is possible. Ask yourself, "Why not me?" Raise your level of ambition.

Aim high. To be the best, aim above the rest. Take the risk. Go where no person has gone before. Be the trailblazer. Other people will follow you.

> *"A great pleasure in life is doing what people say you cannot do."*
>
> *- Walter Gagehot*

Secret #15

You Are More than Enough

Many people fall into the trap of believing they are not good enough.

Stop lying to yourself. You are more than enough.

No matter what life has in store for you, remember you are more than enough. You can handle it.

When someone says you are not qualified, remember you are more than enough. You can develop the qualifications.

No matter what people say to you,

No matter what people do to you,

No matter what happens to you,

Remember you are more than enough.

Secret #16

Seek Out the Top Leaders in Your Field

Find a mentor. Learn from the veterans. Interview people who have years of experience in your field. Take them to lunch. Network with them. Listen to their stories and wisdom. Learn from their mistakes.

Ask them questions.

What would they do differently?

What would they do if they were starting their career today?

"A single conversation across the table with a wise man is worth a month's study of books."

- Chinese proverb

www.JerryPoe.com

Secret #17

Build a Support Team

Create a team of people who support your goals, vision, and dreams from within the faculty and staff at your school. Find individuals who are interested in your success. This will establish an extended or surrogate family for you. The more people you have close by who are encouraging and cheering for you, the better.

> *"No man is an island unto himself. Every man is a piece of the continent, a part of the main."*
>
> *- John Donne*

Secret #18

Be a Thermostat, Not a Thermometer

A Thermometer is changed by the temperature of the environment it is in.

A Thermostat changes the temperature of the environment it is in.

What type of leader are you?

How do you impact your environment?

As a leader you must be a catalyst for change in a positive, productive direction. Do not allow the situation you walked into to lower your standard. Become the Thermostat and set the standard everyone else will adjust to.

"Our life always expresses the result of our dominant thoughts."

- Soren Kierkegaard

Secret #19

Everyone Has Issues

Everyone on this planet has an issue, a problem, or challenge in their life. The faster you realize this fact, the better your life will be.

It is so easy to fall into the trap of thinking you are the only one experiencing problems in life. When it rains, everyone gets wet.

When you feel overwhelmed by your problems in life, remember there is someone on the planet going through the same thing if not something worse.

Everyone is dealing with something. Some people do a better job of hiding what they are dealing with than others.

Always remember it is not just you. You are not the only one dealing with the hard stuff in life.

It happens to the best of us.

Secret #20

Expect the Best and Plan for the Unexpected

Set your attitude for the best possible outcome. Expect your plans to work in your favor. Even though you plan and expect the best, things may not go as smoothly as planned. To be successful, plan for the unexpected. Have a secondary option.

Anticipate different scenarios and plan for them as well. Give yourself extra time to complete projects to cover any surprises or interruptions.

"How you prepare indicates what you expect and determines what you produce." – JFP

"Shooting for the top will bring out the best that's in you."

- Earl Nightingale

Secret #21

Get to Know the Librarian

Build a connection with the librarians in the school library or libraries.

Learn how to use the resources available in the library.

Even though many things are available online and can be utilized remotely, having a face-to-face contact always helps. Plus, you have no idea what resources you are missing if there is no online version of them.

Schedule two to three days a week to visit the library.

"If we knew what it was we were doing, it would not be called research, would it?"

- Albert Einstein

www.JerryPoe.com

Secret #22

Keep the Peace

Create a drama-free environment in life. Eliminate the emotional vampires in your life. Remember you are the author of your life experience. What type of story are you writing?

What are you allowing to affect you?

Who are you allowing to affect you?

Do not allow yourself to be governed by your emotions. Keep your emotions in check. Develop emotional wisdom.

"I can't change the direction of the wind, but I can adjust my sails to always reach my destination."

- Jimmy Dean

Secret #23

You Have a Contract to Fulfill

Everyone has a purpose for their life. You were destined to make a positive impact (large or small) on this planet. You were not born by chance. There is a reason why you are here.

Your purpose, your destiny, your positive impact is your contract to fulfill. Are you going to accept the challenge? Are you going to hold up your end of the deal?

You were given life. Therefore you received the benefits of the contract. Your part of the contract is to do something with your life. Make a positive difference on some level.

"A man without a purpose is like a ship without a rudder."

- Thomas Carlyle

Secret #24

Make the Maximum Your Minimum

Cultivate the mindset of going beyond the minimum effort. Set your standard of production to be the maximum output. What would be the maximum for everyone else now becomes your minimum. Go the extra step. Do more than is required. Always strive to do better than your best. Keep raising your standard of success.

"Excellence means when a man or a woman asks of himself more than others do."

- Ortega Y Gasset

www.JerryPoe.com

Secret #25

Student = Customer

Develop the proper perspective when dealing with your academic institution. As a student you are the customer and the school is the service provider. Make sure you get your return on investment. Do not let anyone shortchange you, including yourself. Respectfully demand the best from everyone you interact with. Take advantage of every asset the institution has to offer.

Become proactive. Make sure you get the full value from the institution.

> *"It is not enough to have a good mind; the main thing is to use it well."*
>
> *- Rene Descartes*

Secret #26

Function Assertively

In all your interactions with people, the key ingredient is to be assertive. When you function assertively, you are behaving in a manner that has the best interest of all parties involved.

You want to make sure they get what they want, and you get what you want; therefore everybody will be content. You show respect. When you do so, you respect others as well as yourself.

You are not going to allow someone else's agenda to infringe on your own; however, you are not going to infringe on someone else's agenda to make sure you achieve your own.

There is an old expression, "You can catch more flies with honey than with vinegar." A person who functions assertively knows to communicate in a way that enables the other person to hear the benefit for themselves in what you are asking them to do.

Secret #27

Elements of Victory

- **V**ision
- **I**ntegrity
- **C**onfidence
- **T**enacity
- **O**ptimism
- **R**esilience
- **Y**ou

Everyone has the ability to create and activate a vision, maintain integrity, increase confidence, develop tenacity, cultivate optimism, and build resilience.

Vision - the act or the power of anticipating that which will or may come to be.

A lack of vision will cause you to have a disempowered life. Where there is a vision, people will prosper. You want to do everything in your power to develop your ability to have vision.

Integrity - the consistency of actions, values, methods, measures, and principles.

Having integrity is honoring your word as yourself. If you are honoring your word, then when you give your word, you stick to it. When people know you as someone who is honest, someone who is moral, then your actions and your words align with each other. This would be walking in integrity.

Confidence - the belief in yourself and your abilities.

Tenacity - a persistent determination.

Optimism - the tendency to expect the best—or at least a favorable—outcome.

Resilience - the ability to recover from or adjust to misfortune or change.

How quickly can you bounce back when things are not going your way? Do you stay in the dumps? Do you stay in a rut for a long period of time? Are you able to snap out of it?

You are the variable. What are you doing on a daily basis to develop, improve, and maintain these areas in your life?

Secret #28

Act like You've Been There Before

Even if you are new to a career or an opportunity, act like you belong there. Make decisions and choices based on how a successful person in your career would behave.

Do not be surprised by your success or achievement. Yes, celebrate and be grateful; however, expect success to be normal for you.

When you act like you belong, then you feel like you belong.

"Where you've been is not half as important as where you're going."

– Anonymous

Secret #29

Party in Moderation

Have fun. Enjoy your youth. Live in the present.

Never forget about the future.

Yes, you can have too much of a good thing—especially when it comes to partying. Keep things in perspective. Know your limits. Remember everyone has their own concept of fun. Set your own boundaries and standards.

"Don't let what you want and what feels good hurt you." –JFP

"People pay for what they do, and still more, for what they have allowed themselves to become. And they pay for it simply: by the lives they lead."

- Edith Wharton

Secret #30

Become an Effective Communicator

The communication process has two sides: there will always be a sender and a receiver. Regardless of what side you are on, as a leader you must remember the most important part of the process is that the message has to be understood.

Hearing is not the same as understanding. As a leader, take responsibility to make sure the message is understood and communication actually took place.

Ask for feedback when you are speaking (the sender), and ask for clarification when you are listening (the receiver).

Be conscious of your body language and tonality. Both have a significant impact on the way a message is understood.

Secret #31

Life Is Choice Driven

Your life is a reflection of your choices. For every choice there is a consequence. You are living out the consequences of all the choices you have made up to this moment in time.

- Choice = Consequence

Remember everything in life is a choice. You may not like the consequences; however, you still have the power to choose.

The choices you make today will shape the future you live in tomorrow.

"When you make a choice ... you must include the consequences." – JFP

"You are where you are today because you've chosen to be there."

- Harry Browne

Secret #32

Model the People Who Have the Results You Want

Results speak for themselves. If you like the results a person is producing, then find out what strategies they are using. Learn the principles and techniques behind their success. What is their system or routine? What are their habits?

You do not need direct contact with a person to model their results. Read their books. Listen to their audio programs. Watch their video courses. Attend their events. Research them. Find out as much about them as possible. What is their story?

"A wise man will make more opportunities than he finds."

- Francis Bacon

Secret #33

Recognize that the College System Is Designed to Help You, but Only if You Use It

The purpose of the college system is to educate and graduate productive individuals.

If you need a tutor ... find one.

If you need help with study skills ... ask about workshops.

Become familiar with the student support services at your school.

The support services are there for a reason, so use them.

"Things may come to those who wait, but only the things left by those who hustle."

- Abraham Lincoln

Secret #34

Control Your Emotions

If you are not in control of your emotions or yourself, then however you feel at that moment in time will determine what you do:

- Whether you respond or react.
- Whether you have a positive or negative outlook.

If you are in control of your emotions and yourself, then regardless of how you feel, you will be able to achieve the result you desire.

"Emotions are neutral; it's what we do with them that can be positive or negative." – JFP

"Anger is never without a reason, but seldom a good one."

- Benjamin Franklin

Secret #35

The Questions Are the Answers

When you ask yourself a question, your brain will provide an answer.

When you ask, "What is wrong?" your brain will find something wrong to provide you an answer.

When you ask, "Why me?" your brain will find a reason to give you.

Start to ask yourself empowering questions. Instead of "What is wrong?" ask "What happened?" or "What can I learn from this?" Instead of "Why me?" ask "How can this refine or improve me?"

"When you change the questions you ask yourself, you change the answers you get." – JFP

Secret #36

Operate in Excellence

You want to be exceptional. You want to be thought of as operating on a higher level than everyone else.

Operating in excellence does not mean you are perfect. It means you have a higher standard than the average person.

The standard you set for yourself will ultimately establish your reputation. What do you want to be known for?

Be known for your attention to details.

Be known for always being prepared.

Be known for going the extra mile.

Be known for getting it done and getting it right.

Secret #37

Listen to Your Adviser; However, Take Control of Your Schedule and Course Selection

Ultimately only you know your goals and desires in life. Let the adviser give advice, not make decisions for you. You know yourself better than anyone else.

When do you want to take classes?

What courses are you interested in?

Set your schedule based on what type of person you are: do you have more energy in the morning, afternoon, or evening?

"Many receive advice, only the wise profit from it."

- Syrus

Secret #38

Listen More than You Speak

Listening is an undervalued aspect of communication. To become a successful leader, listening is a skill you will need to develop.

Remember you were given two ears and one mouth. As a good rule of thumb, listen twice as much as you speak.

Listening helps you understand other people's points of view.

Listening is a way to show empathy.

Listening allows you become more informed about an issue before you share your opinion or make a decision.

"All doors open to courtesy."

- Thomas Fuller

Secret #39

Live Victoriously

Understand you are a victorious person. Expect victory in every area of your life.

Think Victory.

Speak Victory.

Walk in Victory.

Know that Victory is yours every day of your life.

"*Expect victory and you make victory.*"

- *Preston Bradley*

Secret #40

Interview as Much as Possible

Go on as many interviews as you possibly can. Go on interviews if only to get live practice.

Interviewing is a skill. The more practice you have, the better you will be. Get good at fielding questions and articulating your value.

The more interviews you go through, the more natural you will be.

> **"Always do your best. What you plant now, you will harvest later."**
>
> **- Og Mandino**

Secret #41

Do Not Be Ashamed to Ask for Help

Asking for help does not mean you are incapable. We all have strengths and weaknesses. Find someone who is strong in the area where you are having issues or challenges. Ask them for help or assistance to gain support as you navigate through your studies. You do not need to figure everything out on your own.

> **"Experience teaches slowly and at the cost of mistakes."**
>
> **- James A. Froude**

Secret #42

Build Resilience

"Success is not determined by how high you go up the ladder. A true measure of success is how high you bounce when you fall off." – JFP

Will you get up more times than you are knocked down?

To be resilient is to be flexible, quick to recover, resistant, and durable. If you are resilient, you have the ability to handle a high level of difficulty, frustration, and stress.

When facing a storm in life, act like the palm tree. The palm tree will survive the hurricane because it can bend with the wind. The palm tree is so flexible it can become parallel with the ground. Once the storm is over and the wind stops blowing, it snaps right back up into place.

How much can you endure? Can you keep going when it looks dark and there is no light at the end of the tunnel?

www.JerryPoe.com

Secret #43

Your Past Does Not Determine Your Future

What is done is done. You cannot go back and change it. However, you can impact your future based on the action you take today. Break the chains the past has on you. If you allow the past to influence or shape your present, then your future will be the same as your past.

You have the ability to rewrite the script or story of your life. You are the producer, director, screenwriter, editor, and actor/actress of your own movie called *Life*. Every day you are alive is another day on the set called Earth. If you do not like the way things are going, change them.

You either accept the way it is or change it to be what you want.

"In life we have two options ... change or accept. Are you working to change it or are you working to accept it?" – JFP

Secret #44

A Job Does Not Make a Career

- Job = Short Term
- Career = Long Term

A job is something people can get stuck in. A career is something people pick to pursue.

- Job = Work
- Career = Profession

Working a job, you are simply punching a clock. To build a career you must commit to lifelong learning.

You decide which one you want to have ... a job or a career.

"Small opportunities are often the beginning of great enterprises."

- Demosthenes

Secret #45

Use the Course Syllabus as a Blueprint for Your Semester

Build your schedule backwards from the end of the semester. Breakdown the syllabus into check points from the final to the midterm to the start of the semester. Turn the months into weeks and the weeks into daily check points. This will enable you to stay on track throughout the semester.

> *"Concentrate all your thoughts upon the work at hand. The sun's rays do not burn until brought to a focus."*
>
> *- Alexander Graham Bell*

Secret #46

Always Increasing

Always ask yourself this question, "Even though I did succeed today, how do I do it better next time?"

There is always something that can improve in your life. There is always an area of improvement. As long as you are alive, that is a day to get better.

You do not want to stay at the same level and reach a plateau. The reality of the situation is what got you to where you are in life will not keep you there.

If you only keep doing the same thing, eventually the results will start to fade and you won't be able to maintain your current level of success.

It is a game you play—challenge yourself by looking for areas of improvement in every area of your life.

Even if you get to a certain level in one area, well, in these other areas, what could you do to improve them?

Your family life, your personal life, your professional life, your spiritual life—in what areas do you need to improve?

Always look for ways to move up or go to the next level. The whole focus is going to the next level in life.

> *"The speed of the leader determines the rate of the pack."*
>
> *- Ralph Waldo Emerson*

Secret #47

Today Is a New Day

Yesterday is over. Tomorrow has not happened. All you have is Today. Each morning you wake up, you are given a refreshed set of 24 hours (1,440 minutes or 86,400 seconds). It is up to you as to how you use this gift. Ask yourself, "How is today going to be different from yesterday?" Make the most of your day because a new one is not guaranteed tomorrow.

"It is a new day. New possibilities. New opportunities. What are you doing to make today better than yesterday?" – JFP

"Any man's life will be filled with constant and unexpected encouragement if he makes up his mind to do his level best each day."

- Booker T. Washington

Secret #48

Take Responsibility for Your Career

A surefire way to sabotage your career is to expect someone else to look out for you.

The company is focused on the company.

Your coworkers are focused on their careers, their families, and their lives.

Where does that leave you?

At the end of the day, your advancement and your income are all within your responsibility. If you do not take responsibility for your career, who will?

"The highest reward for a person's toil is not what they get for it, but what they become by it."

- John Ruskin

www.JerryPoe.com

Secret #49

Realize the Impact of Being a Student Worker

Do you suffer from too many jobs?

Having money in your pocket as a student is important. However, the primary reason you are at the educational institution is not to work a bunch of part-time jobs.

Make sure the job is not negatively impacting your schoolwork. Do you have enough time for your primary function at the school? Remember you are a student first and a worker second. Keep your priorities straight.

It is possible to work too much.

"We know what happens to people who stay in the middle of the road. They get run over."

- Aneurin Bevan

Secret #50

Appreciate the Process

Everything in life has a process. Sometimes we think it is taking too long to go through a process.

Appreciate where you are in life. Understand there is a reason for why you are where you are.

Remember:

- Patience
- Perseverance
- Protection

Develop patience. Be patient with yourself, others, and life. Cultivate perseverance. Stick with it; hang in until completion. Activate a protection plan. You must protect yourself from people who tell you it is time to quit. There are going to be people who tell you, "Listen, your process is already over."

The optimal results only come from going through a complete process. If you cut the process off too early, you are not going to reach your full potential.

www.JerryPoe.com

Secret #51

Some Friends Do Not Have Your Best Interest in Mind

Be aware of the fact that certain individuals care more about themselves than they ever will about you.

This does not mean you have to walk around guarded or with a wall up. Simply qualify people before you share everything with them. Let their actions determine their status in your life.

There are different levels of friendly relationships:

- Friend
- Associate
- Acquaintance

Not every relationship qualifies for the same benefits, trust, and disclosure.

Secret #52

Everyone Is Self-Employed

- Self = Personal interest
- Employed = Put to use

Your employment status is up to you. You decide what job or position you will accept. You decide what income level you will take. We are all working for ourselves regardless of whether you have a job or a business. You do not show up to work for the company's benefit; you show up for your own benefit.

Who are you working for?

Once you realize you are self-employed, you need to act like a self-employed person would act.

- Be a self-starter
- Take the initiative
- Invest in your skill sets
- Have the mindset of the owner

www.JerryPoe.com

Secret #53

Always Sit in the Front Row

Where are the best seats on an airplane?

First Class is up front and it is where you get the most attention.

Why do people want to be ringside at a fight or courtside at a game?

They want to be close to the action.

The same can be said for the classroom. You want the attention of the instructor. You want him/her to know you are present. Sit up front. You want to be where the action is taking place during the instruction so that you do not miss anything. Sit up front.

Being in the front of the room causes you to pay more attention to the instructor because you are less distracted by what else is going on in the room.

Sitting in the front makes a statement about how serious you are as a student. It will make a positive impression on the instructor as well.

The best seats are always in the front of the room. Be where the action is.

"Achieve success in any area of life by identifying the optimum strategies and repeating them until they become habits."

- Karl Wilhelm von Humboldt

www.JerryPoe.com

Secret #54

Maintain Equilibrium

Life is balance. In order to prevent ourselves from getting burnt out or totally wiped out, we have to maintain some level of balance.

Everything in life is about ups and downs, highs and lows, the yin and the yang. There's a balance to everything.

Being a successful leader means learning how to maintain equilibrium. Math is all about equilibrium. One side of the equation has to match the other side of the equation. Everything has to balance out.

In life, people think they can keep their lives out of balance for an extended period of time without any repercussions. You can only go at 100 miles an hour for so long before you run out of gas.

You need to focus the same amount of time on producing a result as you spend on relaxing and recuperating.

Without balance, things will break down.
If there is no equilibrium, things fall
apart.

> **"A jest often decides matters
> of importance more
> effectually and happily than
> seriousness."**
>
> **- Horace**

Secret #55

Guard Your Mind

Your brain goes through different states throughout the day. In certain states the brain is more susceptible to suggestion. When your guard is down, you are more open to being influenced.

- Alpha - most alert point
- Beta - awake, but zoned out
- Theta - half awake, half asleep
- Delta - deep sleep

When you are not fully alert, your conscious guard is down, which allows information to move directly to the subconscious. What are you exposing yourself to in those points and times in your day? How are your attitude, outlook, and expectation being shaped by what you watch, listen to, and read?

Do something radical ...

Shut off the television. When you shut the TV off, you are going to realize how much time you actually have in your day. TV is a time killer.

Turn off the radio. Listen to an uplifting audio.

Secret #56

Dress the Part

Appearance does matter.

Dress for the career or position you want, rather than the one you have.

Use the company dress code as a guide, not your standard. If business causal is the norm, then dress one step above business causal. There is a difference between khaki pants and dress slacks. The minor attention to details and style make a huge impact on the impression people have of you.

"Start by doing what's necessary; then do what's possible; and suddenly you are doing the impossible."

- St. Francis of Assisi

Secret #57

Never Skip a Class

Attendance is an overlooked aspect of success. The simple act of showing up can be the deciding factor in moving a grade level or not. Many professors will give the benefit of the doubt to those who showed up every day when it comes to setting the final grade for the semester.

Class attendance does count.

"The secret of success in life is for a man to be ready for his opportunity when it comes."

- Benjamin Disraeli

Secret #58

Develop Self-Discipline

We will do things because we feel like it, or we will not do something because we do not feel like it. At that moment in time, we may not see the result of that decision.

But doing things based on how you feel over a period of time can lead us to disastrous circumstances.

It is not the one day of doing or not doing; it is doing or not doing over a period of time.

People who are self-disciplined do what needs to be done even when they do not feel like it because they have control over themselves. They have a mastery of self.

Do you do what you are supposed to do because you are supposed to do it, or do you do things because you feel like it?

Throughout our lives, we have to look for areas where we are disciplined versus areas where we are not disciplined. The areas where you do not have discipline will cause you to end up where you do not want to be.

"The level of self-discipline in your life will govern your level of success." – JFP

"Regret for the things we did can be tempered by time; it is regret for the things we did not do that is inconsolable."

- Sydney J Harris

Secret #59

Count Your Victories

Make a Glory File as part of your reflection time. People are going to give you compliments. People are going to write you thank-you letters. You want to collect these things.

A Glory File is an emotional bank account. When you receive thank-you cards, thank-you letters, or compliments (no matter how big or small), keep a record them.

When you are not feeling 100 percent emotionally, you can go back to your Glory File and look at the positive things people have said about you. This will enable you to bring your emotional state to the level you need it to be in order to keep going on.

When you want to change, when you move out of your comfort zone and do things that you have never done before, you are going to start to feel opposition.

Tapping into the emotional bank account will help you keep pushing forward. Reflecting on some of those positive things people have said gives us enough energy to keep moving.

"We have a tendency to see our failures ... so often we ignore when we win. Spend more time counting your victories in life than you spend counting your losses." – JFP

"I long to accomplish some great and noble task, but it is my chief duty to accomplish small tasks as if they were great and noble."

- Helen Keller

Secret #60

Early Is Better than Late

What impression do you create when you are five minutes late?

What impression do you create when you are five minutes early?

Which impression would you rather create?

Set your clock or watch 10 minutes ahead. This way you will always arrive ahead of schedule. It is better for you to wait for a meeting to start because you are early than it would be for others to wait to start a meeting because you are late.

"Punctuality is the politeness of kings and the duty of gentle people everywhere."

- Anonymous

Secret #61

Study with Those Who Are Smarter than You

Look for and find study groups with the top people in your class. Their grades are proof they are doing something right. Spend time learning from them and studying with them. This will enable you to pick up and develop habits to produce higher grades than you currently have.

Find study groups or partners.

"My great concern is not whether you have failed, but whether you are content with your failure."

- Abraham Lincoln

Secret #62

Be a Person of Character

Character - moral or ethical quality

Leaders are people of great character.

How do you act behind closed doors?

How do you act in public?

Which one is the real you?

A person's character is tested when the stress level is high and the pressure is on. This is when you see the true character of a person.

"Your name is only as good as your word and your character." – JFP

"Your rewards will be determined by the extent of your contribution, that is your service to others."

- Earl Nightingale

www.JerryPoe.com

Secret #63

Feed Your Mind

Expose your mind to something positive by reading something positive, uplifting, and empowering for at least 15 minutes every single day.

"When you transform your thought life, you can step into your future and claim your destiny." – JFP

"I would rather be an optimist and proven a fool than to be a pessimist and be proven right."

- Anonymous

Secret #64

Remember Life Is a Stage

You never know who is watching or listening. You need to be conscious of your attitude and behavior everywhere you go. A potential contact or employer might be right next to you.

You are always auditioning for the next opportunity. You never know who knows whom. The conversation you are currently having could be with the person who leads you to your next career opportunity.

With technology, anyone can now capture audio and video of you that will be around forever. Be aware of the image you are creating and how it will impact your career.

"The actions of men are the best interpreters of their thoughts."

- John Locke

Secret #65

Have a Graduation Focus

Make graduation your primary focus. Everything you do and whatever you participate in should be moving you toward graduation.

Evaluate all your activities.

Evaluate all the opportunities presented to you.

Ask yourself, "Will this activity or opportunity move me closer to graduation or take me away from it?"

Having graduation as your primary focus will enable you to set your priorities properly.

"The best way to predict the future is to create it."

- Peter Drucker

Secret #66

Be Unreasonable

As a leader there will be times when you commit to something you realize you do not really want to do. There will be times when you over-commit.

It is at these moments that you will start to create reasons to excuse reneging or wiggling out somehow. You can come up with tons of reasons for why you cannot do it.

Start reversing the process. Instead of allowing the reasons to stop you from fulfilling the commitment, become unreasonable. Get past the reasons. Eliminate the reasons. Overcome the reasons.

Better yet ... find reasons why you should fulfill the commitment.

"Live your life around your commitments, not your commitments around your life." - JFP

Secret #67

Take an Account of Your Day

At the end of your day, take about 30 minutes to reflect. This could be prayer time, it could be meditation, and it could be time for you to give affirmations.

What you want to do in this reflection time is focus on the good, focus on what you have, focus on what you will have, and give thanks. You want to start to cultivate an attitude of gratitude.

Start a journal. Every day list 10 things that you are grateful for.

"Life is largely a matter of expectation."

- Horace

Secret #68

Join Student Organizations That Are Right for You

There are many organizations at your school. All of them are great; however, all are not right for you.

When you are picking which groups to join, think about how the organization will impact and empower you to grow and develop—as a person, as a leader, and as a student.

You want to think about what you will bring to the group. But the more important factors are ...

Who you will become?

How will you improve?

What you will learn?

... as a result of membership.

Join the right organizations.

Secret #69

You Are Responsible

Being a leader means taking responsibility. Take responsibility for the team. Take responsibility for your life.

When you take responsibility, you recognize you are a cause of whatever consequence or result happens, whether it is in life or with the team.

Knowing you are responsible empowers you to make changes for the better rather than blaming someone or something else for your circumstances.

Whatever comes your way ... good or bad ... positive or negative, remember you are responsible. Change starts with you, not the other person or thing.

"The price of greatness is responsibility."

- Sir Winston Churchill

Secret #70

You Were Born a Winner

How do I know you were born a winner? Because you are alive, thinking, and breathing. For you to show up on this planet, you had to be a winner. Because in order to show up, you had to win a race. Everybody who showed up here won a race. There were over a million other little swimming cells trying to get to the egg. You won! Therefore you are a winner.

"When you see yourself as a victorious person, it changes the reality you step into, which will enable you to excel on a higher level." – JFP

"No man is free who is not master of himself."

- Epictetus

Secret #71

Remember Your WHY

Always remember why you applied in the first place. Why did you want to go to college? What do you want to gain from the experience? What will your education do for you? How will it benefit you long term?

When things get tough, turn to your reason WHY to help re-energize you.

Your reason WHY **W**ill **H**elp **Y**ou stay motivated.

Your reason WHY is **W**hat **H**olds **Y**ou up when you fall down.

Remember WHY you are there.

"Nothing great was ever achieved without enthusiasm."

- Ralph Waldo Emerson

Secret #72

Never Stop Investing in Yourself

As a leader you set the standard for the team. Your level of growth and development put a cap on the team level of growth and development.

If you do not continue to learn, educate, grow, and develop yourself as a leader, you will create limitations for your team members.

Either they will follow your lead and not learn, educate, grow, and develop, or they will outgrow you and look for another leader.

You want to eliminate both of these options from happening. Become a lifelong learner. Become a continual student of life.

"Happy are those who dream dreams and are willing to pay the price to make them come true."

– Anonymous

Secret #73

Everyone You Know Is Not Your Friend

Be careful who you associate with. Some people are dream stealers and emotional vampires.

Limit your time with negative and disempowering people. Avoid complainers and criticizers. Get to know someone with a great attitude, and model yourself after him or her.

You do not have to cut people off. You do not have to be rude or negative or anything like that. But you know that every person you deal with has a certain amount of positivity inside them. You can give them that amount of time.

Certain people will talk to you for two minutes and then start going through some negative stuff. After those two minutes, you have to go. You do not let them know you gave them two minutes; you can exit respectfully.

Secret #74

Inspect What You Expect

As a successful leader you must monitor the progress of those you lead. You cannot expect people to always know how to do something simply because you know how to do it.

If you have a certain expectation, then at some point you need to make an inspection.

Determine if the process is being followed properly.

Is the team on track to meet the deadline?

Do team members need more instruction or understanding of the process?

Do not be caught off-guard by an unexpected result. Make sure you check in to see how things are going. The more you monitor the process, the more you can control the outcome.

Secret #75

You Are Stronger than You Realize

The amount of limitations people put on themselves is amazing. You would be shocked by how much more you can accomplish if you push yourself to the limit.

There is a tendency to cap the strength or potential of our physical body. However, your heart and mind can cause the body to endure more than what we think is humanly possible.

You will never know how much you can really do until you push yourself past the discomfort.

Once you break through the discomfort (the wall), a whole new possibility of what you are capable of now exists.

Break down the walls of your limitations today.

Secret #76

Your Actions Are Speaking. What Are They Saying?

People pay more attention to what you do than what you say. What message are you sending as a leader?

Those who follow your leadership will be a reflection of you and what you do. Your words can only go so far. Eventually people will watch your walk and stop listening to your talk.

Lead with your actions, not your words.

What example are you setting? One to avoid or one to imitate?

"So live that you wouldn't be ashamed to sell the family parrot to the town gossip."

- Will Rogers

www.JerryPoe.com

Secret #77

People Are Meaning-Making Machines

Part of being human is the need to understand things. People create meanings or making meanings of things that happen to them in life. Many times people create meanings for things that have no meaning.

Someone did not call you. What does it mean?

Someone did not speak to you this morning. What does it mean?

It has to mean something. Right?

The problem is you create meanings which are usually negative or disempowering.

If you are going to make up something, why not make up something positive or empowering?

Because you are making up all these meanings yourself, create ones that will serve you rather than be a disservice.

Ideas and Insights

www.JerryPoe.com

Ideas and Insights

Empower and Equip Others!
Share this Book

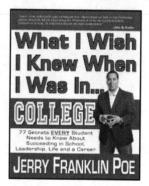

What I Wish I Knew When I Was in ... College

77 Secrets EVERY Student Needs to Know about Succeeding in School, Leadership, Life, and a Career

How great would it be if you were given a manual to guide you through every aspect of your life that lay ahead of you? Give yourself the winning edge. Crack the code to success in school, leadership, life, and a career by reading the tips shared throughout this book. These quick tips are easy to read, understand, and more importantly apply immediately. Go ahead and get started!

Special Quantity Discounts

2 – 20 Books	**$15.00**
21 – 99 Books	**$14.00**
100 – 499 Books	**$13.00**
500 – 999 Books	**$12.00**
1000+ Books	**$11.00**

To Place an Order
Call (484) 301-0763

www.JerryPoe.com